Could You Love Me Like My™ Cat?

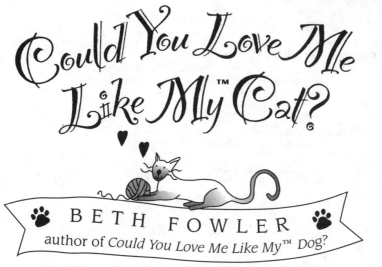

BETH FOWLER

author of *Could You Love Me Like My™ Dog?*

A FIRESIDE BOOK PUBLISHED BY SIMON & SCHUSTER

FIRESIDE
Rockefeller Center
1230 Avenue of the Americas
New York, NY 10020

Library of Congress Cataloging-in-Publication Data
Fowler, Beth.
 Could you love me like my cat? / Beth Fowler.
  p. cm.
 1. Cats—Miscellanea. I. Title.
 SF445.5.F68 1996
 818'.5407—dc20   96-2954
          ISBN 0-684-81901-5

Beth Fowler is the owner of the trademarks
"COULD YOU LOVE ME LIKE MY™" and "I PURR FOR YOU™"

Special thanks to those whose encouragement made this book possible:

Alice, Amy, Andrea, Anita, Ann, B, Bi, Big Bill, Bill, Bob, Brad, Carla, Carol, Carolyn, Chris, Cindy, David, Debbie, Dudley, Edward, Ellie, George, Glen, Graham, Joan, Kevin, Kim, Laura, Laurie, Lisa, Louise, Lynn, Mame, Mark, Mary, Mary Jayne, May May, Merrimac, Mike, Misty, Neal, Patricia, Pauline, Read, Roberta, Rose, Sally, and Shelley.

Dedicated to my nephew, Will,
who learned to love,
and still misses,
his orange-and-white cat
named Longhorn.

Introduction

If you have ever had a cat, you know cats love subtly, with nuances that could easily be missed. Maybe cats are here to teach us how to recognize these signs.

My first childhood love was a Siamese cat named Smoky. She raced through the house, climbed up my father's bare leg, and over the years bore many black kittens, each of which my brother named John Henry. At night, Smoky snuggled into my arms and hummed me to sleep.

.   Ten years ago, a lost Siamese kitten appeared in my window. I quickly adopted her, and she agreed to be called Ming. She warmed my lap and nestled in as a constant companion. The way she loves is quiet and gentle, and if a love like that ever crept into my heart on two legs as softly as those little cat feet, I'd be purring for the rest of my life.

Wouldn't you, if someone loved you like your cat?

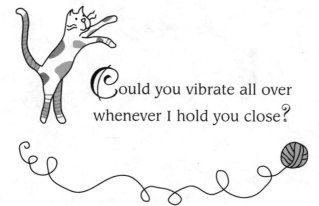

Could you vibrate all over whenever I hold you close?

5

Could you hang loose?

Could you concentrate so hard on what I'm saying that sometimes your eyes get crossed?

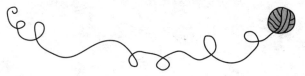

Could you touch me gently
whenever you walk by?

8

Could you always be mysterious?

Could you forgive me if I accidentally lock you out and you have to sleep under the car?

Could you never get your back up at me?

11

Could you crane your neck around corners and doorways to make sure you don't bump into me?

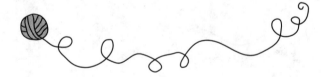

12

Could you not mind when
I say you have fish breath?

Could you wave at me from under doors
and dust ruffles and shower curtains?

Could you ask for what you want?

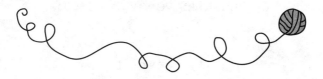

Could you let me swoop you
up and cover you with kisses?

Could you always smell good?

17

Could you bring me small tokens of your affection like lizards and beetles and flies?

Could you melt into my arms?

Could you always warm up the bed for me?

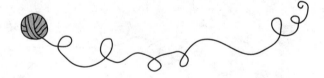

Could you play hide-and-seek between the sheets?

Could you be graceful under pressure
and always land on your feet?

Could you crouch and flex your
muscles before you pounce on me?

23

Could you not be ashamed
of looking in the mirror?

Could you walk away from your mistakes?

Could you always be soft and fuzzy whenever I want a hug?

Could you show your interest in my daily activities by shoving your head into my shoes?

*C*ould you accept appreciation?

Could you be supportive of my work
by staying on top of what I'm doing?

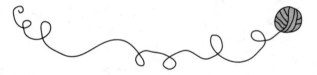

Could you perk up your ears to
show you're always listening?

30

Could you wink at me?

31

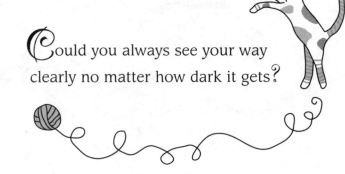

Could you always see your way clearly no matter how dark it gets?

32

Could you be self-reliant?

Could you be curious about anything new?

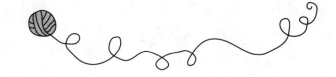

Could you never get enough of my affection?

35

Could you sprawl across me whenever
I'm reading or watching TV?

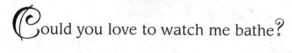

Could you love to watch me bathe?

37

Could you tell me it's time to get up by purring in my ear?

Could you let me know if
I rub you the wrong way?

$\mathcal{C}$ould you be willing to bat anything around?

40

Could you appreciate nature and savor fresh blades of grass?

Could you surprise me?

Could you announce it's spring by gagging and choking up hairballs?

43

Could you just skulk out of sight
whenever you're in a bad mood?

Could you never hiss at me?

Could you keep me interested
by playing hard to get?

Could you be considerate and not hog the bed by sleeping curled up in a tight little ball?

47

Could you trust me enough
to let me rub your tummy?

Could you not be needy or dependent?

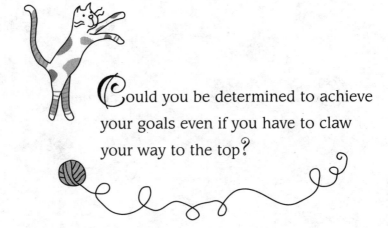

Could you be determined to achieve your goals even if you have to claw your way to the top?

Could you appreciate peace and quiet?

51

Could you maneuver out of any tight spot by cocking your head and squeezing through one shoulder at a time?

Could you arch your back and become
mesmerized whenever I stroke your spine?

53

Could you wash up after every meal?

54

Could you always warm my heart?

Could you never get tired of staring at me?

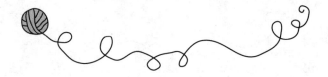

Could you observe newcomers from a distance and never rush new friendships?

Could you always follow the sun?

Could you be ready to snuggle up anytime and take a nap with me?

59

Could you let me burrow my face in your chest?

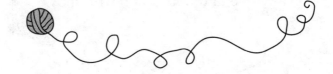

Could you let me tangle you up in string?

Could you gently massage the kinks out by walking on my back?

Could you have confidence
and high self-esteem?

Could you enhance the decor by posing
on windowsills and steps and mantels?

Could you stay in shape by sprinting through the house?

Could you be dainty and well mannered when you eat?

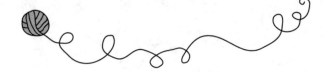

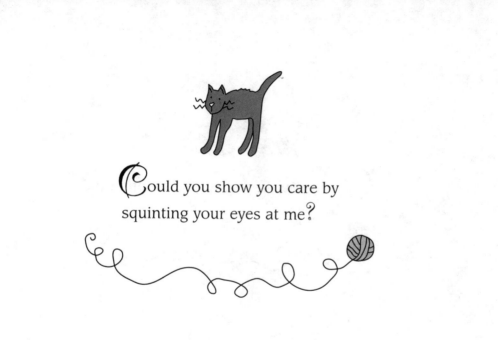

Could you show you care by
squinting your eyes at me?

67

Could you drape yourself around me?

Could you let me put a bell on you
so I always know where you are?

$\mathcal{C}$ould you maintain your own
identity and unique personality?

70

Could you seek new heights?

Could you keep me on my toes by
weaving in and out between my feet?

Could you watch out for me from the window?

Could you never be too much
of a burden for me to carry?

74

Could you amaze me with your agility?

Could you do the dusting with
a gentle swish of your tail?

76

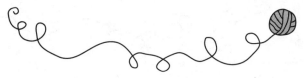

Could you entice me to chase you through the house in a game of cat and mouse?

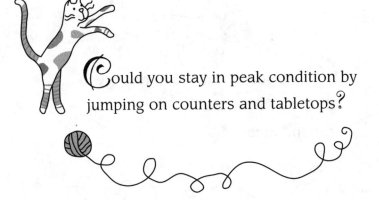

Could you stay in peak condition by jumping on counters and tabletops?

Could you always reach for my hand?

Could you not mind if I unintentionally
shut you in the closet?

Could you have a vivid imagination?

81

Could you always notice unusual noises
and things that go bump in the night?

82

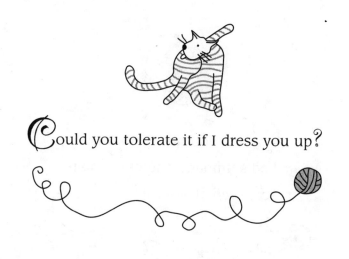

Could you tolerate it if I dress you up?

83

Could you not mind if the bed's unmade and clothes are scattered all over it?

84

Could you never yowl at me,
even when you're miffed?

85

Could you accept it if I insist on separate bathrooms?

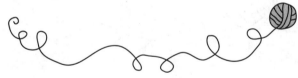

Could you show you're feeling threatened by standing your hair on end and puffing up to twice your size?

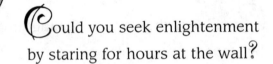

Could you seek enlightenment
by staring for hours at the wall?

88

Could you stretch yourself?

Could you perch above me
and peer into my eyes?

90

Could you be prepared for anything
by getting plenty of rest?

91

Could you like my clothes so much that sometimes you even get stuck to them?

Could you make yourself comfortable
no matter where you are?

93

Could you let me pick you up and cuddle you?

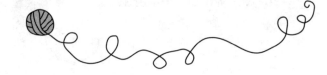

94

Could you never drool?

Could you protect my favorite sweaters from getting holes in them by leaping up and swatting moths?

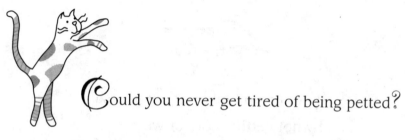

Could you never get tired of being petted?

 97

Could you take care of yourself
by not getting cold or wet?

Could you enjoy my company?

$\mathcal{C}$ould you always be sleek and sensual?

Could you help me relax by kneading my neck and shoulders?

Could you pad softly around the room whenever you wake up before me?

Could you help with the sewing
by pulling off loose buttons?

Could you persevere and never
take no for an answer?

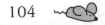

104

Could you master physics by studying
the flight of birds and insects?

 105

Could you make sure we get good bargains by counting the sheets on rolls of toilet paper?

 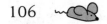

Could you always be light on your feet?

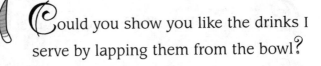

Could you show you like the drinks I serve by lapping them from the bowl?

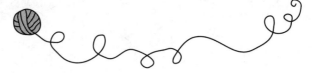

Could you fight off going stir-crazy
by dashing madly from room to room?

109

Could you sneak up on me?

Could you stay limber enough to tuck your head into your feet?

 111

Could you pop up anywhere, like in a drawer or a box or a bag?

112

Could you always pay attention
to your grooming?

113

Could you just walk away whenever you're feeling like a sourpuss?

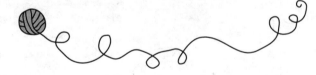

Could you tickle me with your whiskers?

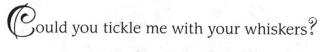

115

Could you eat nutritiously
and drink plenty of milk?

Could you let me know when you're losing patience by glaring and lashing your tail?

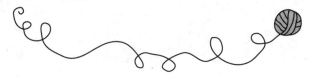

$\mathcal{C}$ould you proudly display for
me whatever you just drug in?

Could you hate so much for me to
leave that you stow away in my suitcase?

119

Could you understand when I need some extra rest and be willing to sleep in?

Could you never stop rubbing
your tail against me?

121

*C*ould you be resourceful?

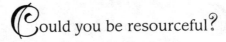

 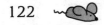

Could you love it when I run
my fingers through your hair?

$\mathcal{C}$ould you always intrigue me?

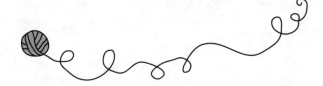

124

Could you be direct and not pussyfoot around?

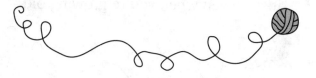

 125

Could you stay the same little kitten inside even when you're growing old?

Could you leave clumps of hair all over
so I remember to do the vacuuming?

 127

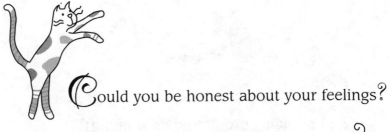

Could you be honest about your feelings?

Could you be meticulous about
scrubbing behind your ears?

129

Could you tell me it's dinnertime
by gently rubbing my ankles?

130

Could you not get mad if sometimes I roll over and squash you in my sleep?

 131

Could you let me know you're there
by lightly patting me on the arm?

132

Could you remind me to take a break
from work by sitting right in my way?

Could you be creative?

 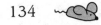

Could you communicate by making eyes at me?

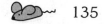 135

Could you be domestic on the outside but a tiger deep inside?

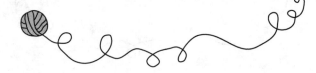

Could you never stop wanting
to crawl into my lap?

Could you make little mewing sounds when you get excited?

138

Could you keep the house bug free?

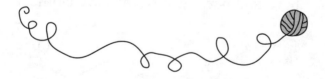

Could you be happy with the coat you have and never want expensive clothes?

Could you investigate nooks and crannies?

Could you pretend to be invisible by flattening yourself against the wall?

 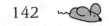

Could you always rumble a special greeting from way down deep?

 143

Could you not let secrets out of the bag?

144

$\mathcal{C}$ould you make sure you stay close to me?

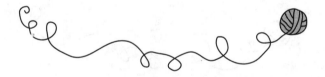

 145

Could you be a dreamer?

146

Could you take care around my breakables?

147

$\mathbb{C}$ould you pursue your own interests?

148

Could you keep your life in balance?

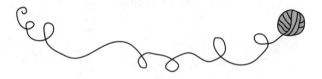

 149

Could you be fun and playful
when you take a little nip?

150

Could you always soothe me?

151

Could you wake me up from nightmares
and make sure that I'm okay?

Could you let me use you as a pillow?

 153

Could you be content?

Could you never take anything too seriously?

 155

Could you be gracious?

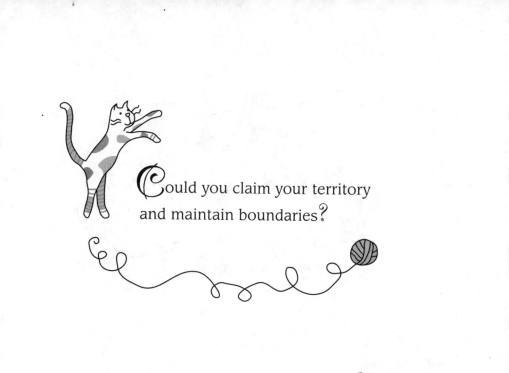

Could you claim your territory
and maintain boundaries?

Could you mark me as your own?

Could you like staying home
with me and never cat around?

 159

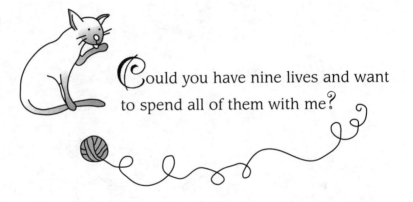

Could you have nine lives and want to spend all of them with me?

160